HAILSTORMS:
CAUSES AND EFFECTS

by Kaitlyn Duling

www.12StoryLibrary.com

12-Story Library is an imprint of Bookstaves.

Developed and produced for 12-Story Library by Focus Strategic Communications Inc.

Library of Congress Cataloging-in-Publication Data
Names: Duling, Kaitlyn, author.
Title: Hailstorms : causes and effects / by Kaitlyn Duling.
Description: Mankato, Minnesota : 12-Story Library, [2022] | Series: Wild weather |
Includes bibliographical references and index. | Audience: Ages 10–13 | Audience: Grades 4–6
Identifiers: LCCN 2020017453 (print) | LCCN 2020017454 (ebook) | ISBN 9781645821489 (library binding) |
ISBN 9781645821861 (paperback) | ISBN 9781645822219 (pdf)
Subjects: LCSH: Hailstorms—Juvenile literature.
Classification: LCC QC929.H15 D85 2022 (print) | LCC QC929.H15 (ebook) | DDC 551.55/4—dc23
LC record available at https://lccn.loc.gov/2020017453
LC ebook record available at https://lccn.loc.gov/2020017454

Photographs ©: Ben Romalis/Shutterstock.com, cover, 1; cdstocks/Shutterstock.com, 4; Andrey Solovev/ Shutterstock.com, 5; National Severe Storms Laboratory(NSSL)/NOAA, 5; Evgenia Parajanian/Shutterstock.com, 6; NOAA, 7; Ken Tannenbaum/Shutterstock.com, 7; Menno van der Haven/Shutterstock.com, 8; Jeff March/Alamy, 9; Scott Alan Ritchie/Shutterstock.com, 9; Happy Owl/Shutterstock.com, 9; Merrimon Crawford/Shutterstock.com, 10; Win Henderson/FEMA, 10; Aviation Club/YouTube.com, 11; Kgbo/CC4.0, 11; Aleksandr Ozerov/Shutterstock.com, 12; Meryll/Shutterstock.com, 13; NARUCHA KLINUDOM/Shutterstock.com, 13; KOAA 5/YouTube.com, 13; Sharaf Maksumov/Shutterstock.com, 14; Jeffery Isaac Greenberg 2/Alamy, 15; Roger Brown Photography/ Shutterstock.com, 15; frans lemmons/Alamy, 16; NOAA/NWS, 17; dvande/Shutterstock.com, 17; Arnold Paul/CC2.5, 18; Laura McCook/Shutterstock.com, 19; Lukas Jonaitis/Shutterstock.com, 19; roseberry3/Shutterstock.com, 20; JeffreyMustard/CC4.0, 21; inga spence/Alamy, 21; mwesselsphotography/Shutterstock.com, 22; NASA, 23; Mark 1333/YouTube.com, 23; Michael Thompson/CC3.0, 24; Shay Levy/Alamy, 25; Marco Kaschuba/YouTube.com, 25; Ben Romalis/Shutterstock.com, 26; Motofoto/Alamy, 27; Walker Art Library/Alamy, 27; Tom Gowanlock/ Shutterstock.com, 28; revers/Shutterstock.com, 29; Pepgooner/Shutterstock.com, 29; ZikG/Shutterstock.com, 29

About the Cover
Large hail stones pound the roof of a car.

Access free, up-to-date content on this topic plus a full digital version of this book. Scan the QR code on page 31 or use your school's login at 12StoryLibrary.com.

Table of Contents

1

What's That Falling from the Sky?

"Clink." "Plink." Hail can be loud on a window or roof. It's not rain. It's not snow. It's little balls of solid ice that fall from the sky. Hailstones are a type of precipitation. They can be clear or cloudy. Some hailstones are as small as a pea, while others are as big as a human hand. Small hailstones fall slowly, at just nine miles per hour (14.5 km/h), but the heaviest hailstones can fall at over 100 miles per hour (160 kph).

Hailstones can be big or small.

Hailstones often damage roofs during a storm.

Hailstones form in the clouds during thunderstorms. Wind carries raindrops up into the cold parts of the atmosphere, where they freeze. Then they collide with water droplets, gaining layers and growing bigger. Eventually, the hailstones become too heavy. The clouds and wind can't hold them. The hail falls to the ground in a hailstorm. Hail can hurt. Hailstorms sometimes damage cars and homes. Luckily, most hailstorms only last a few minutes.

31

Weight in ounces (880 g) of the largest hailstone ever found in the US

- The hailstone measured 8 inches (20 cm) across and 18.6 inches (47 cm) around.
- It fell in Vivian, South Dakota, on June 23, 2010.
- Hail falls in paths called hail swaths.

2

Is Hail the Same as Sleet?

Brrr. Hail is cold. That makes sense because it is frozen. These tiny balls of ice don't usually fall in winter, though. They tend to fall during the warmer seasons. Spring, summer, and fall are the months when we are most likely to see hail.

In the winter, it snows. It rains. And sometimes there is sleet. Sleet occurs when rain or melted snow freezes into ice pellets as it falls from the sky.

Roads are dangerous after sleet.

Hail Formation

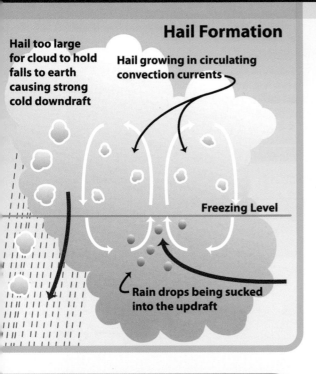

Hail too large for cloud to hold falls to earth causing strong cold downdraft

Hail growing in circulating convection currents

Freezing Level

Rain drops being sucked into the updraft

The ice is light and tiny. It bounces when it hits the ground. Sleet often falls in a mix of freezing rain, snow, and ice pellets. A weather app or weather channel on television might call this "wintry mix." Triple burr.

To remember the difference between sleet and hail, think of this: Sleet forms as it falls from the sky. Hail forms in a cloud. That's all there is to it.

THINK ABOUT IT

Sleet storms are harder to forecast than rain or snowstorms. Why do you think that is?

6

Amount of sleet in inches (15 cm) received during one winter storm in Kentucky and Indiana in December 2004

- The storm included thundersleet.
- During thundersleet, there is thunder and lightning. Sleet falls instead of rain.
- Sleet storms are dangerous. They make roads icy.

What Happens After a Hailstorm?

Hailstorms are quick. They usually last just five to 10 minutes. But they can do plenty of damage in that time. When people step outside, their neighborhood might look like an alien planet. Little balls of ice cover the roads. Debris is everywhere.

After a hailstorm, communities get to work. There is much to be done.

The most dangerous issues are handled first. Hail coats roads in layers of ice. Road crews use plows to clear the roads and make them drivable again. Cars are dug out from

Sometimes so much hail falls that it looks like snow.

icy parking spots. People use shovels to clear the ice in front of their homes. If broken glass covers the ground, it gets cleaned up.

Sometimes hailstorms cause trees and power lines to fall down. The power can go out across an entire neighborhood or town. It takes time and money to clear roads, fix the electricity, and clean up areas affected by hailstorms. They are some of the most expensive weather disasters.

$2.8 billion
Cost of damage for the most expensive hailstorm in US history

- The storm hit Phoenix, Arizona, in October 2010.
- Hailstones measured up to three inches (7.5 cm) across.
- The storm also brought high winds, rain, and flooding.

9

How do Hailstorms Affect Me?

Hail falls fast. The bigger the hailstone, the faster it falls. Zooming hailstones can cause serious damage to cars, airplanes, homes, animals, and people.

Violent hailstorms can cause severe damage to houses and cars.

Most hailstones don't have smooth edges. When large hailstones hit roofs and cars, they leave dents.

When they hit windows, they shatter glass. Softball-size hailstones can even puncture a roof. After a hailstorm, a homeowner may need to replace the entire roof, or worse.

It can be dangerous to drive and walk outside after a hailstorm. Ice coats the road. It coats the sidewalk. Ice is

130

Number of passengers on American Airlines Flight 1897

- In 2018, the plane flew into a violent hailstorm over eastern New Mexico.
- The storm completely destroyed the plane's nose and cracked its windshield.
- The plane landed safely, and no one was hurt.

everywhere. There may be glass on the ground, too. This makes for hazardous conditions.

GROWING COSTS

Experts think that the costs of hailstorms will continue to grow. Why? More people are moving into hail-prone parts of the country. It costs money to fix their homes after hailstorms. Homes have gotten bigger, too. That means there's more potential for damage. Both of these factors create costlier storms.

How Do Hailstorms Affect Natural Environments and Animals?

Plant damage from hail.

Living things need water. They welcome rainfall and can even withstand storms. A hailstorm, on the other hand, can severely damage plants. Gardens, yards, and parks, beware. Hail can strip trees of leaves and fruit. It can pull down branches, completely destroy farmers' crops, and injure livestock.

Farmers and gardeners are *not* fans of hail.

After hail melts, it affects the environment just like rain water. While it can add moisture to plants and the soil, too much water is not a good thing. Melted hail can cause flooding. Over time, too much water causes erosion.

Soil erosion.

THINK ABOUT IT

Do you think pets get scared when it storms? How can you tell?

The water removes soil and rock. Erosion happens on coasts, mountainsides, and other places. Slowly but surely, the landscape changes. Such changes can alter the lives of animals and plants.

11,000
Number of animals killed or injured in a Montana hailstorm in 2019

- The hailstorm hit a lake and nesting area.
- Hailstones measuring two inches (5 cm) rained down at 70 miles per hour (110 km/h)
- Twenty to 30 percent of the birds in the wildlife area were killed by the storm.

How Do We Find Out about Hailstorms?

Extreme weather alerts are sent to cell phones.

A hailstorm is about to hit. People need to be ready. With warning, they can find shelter. They can check on their pets. Farmers can protect their livestock. They can put their cars safely inside garages.

Shutters can be shut to protect windows.

How do people find out about hailstorms? Local weather forecasts are on TV and the radio. They can also be found online. The first storm warning

90

Percent of the time that a five-day forecast is correct

- A 10-day forecast is right only about half of the time.
- Weather satellites orbit between 500 and 22,000 miles (800 and 35,000 km) above Earth.
- Weather balloons only rise to about 24 miles (40 km) above Earth.

was issued in 1860. It was sent by telegraph. These days, most cell phones have apps for weather alerts. Experts use satellites and weather balloons to get data. Computer programs and other tools help them predict the weather.

An emergency kit keeps people prepared for any situation.

GET READY

Sometimes weather reports predict bad hailstorms. When that happens, it can be helpful to have an emergency kit on hand. A kit might include bottled water and canned food. It might have clothing. First aid supplies and a flashlight are helpful, too—and extra batteries.

Is It Going to Hail Today?

Hail storm clouds.

It could hail today. It could hail tomorrow. It may have hailed yesterday. How do we know what to expect? We look to meteorologists. They study weather.

These experts look for three things when they predict hail. First, there must be wind to hold the hail in the air. Second, there must be cold water near the hailstones. That helps them grow larger. Finally, there should be some ice, snow, or dust in the air. That's where the hail starts.

Experts use many tools to look for these three ingredients. One of the most helpful is radar. Radio waves are sent out into the air. Those waves can detect things like snow and water. They can also

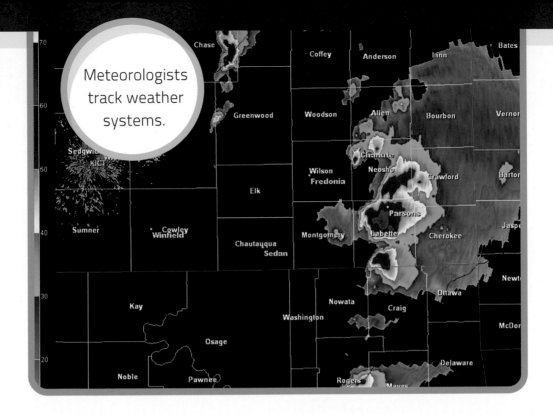

Meteorologists track weather systems.

detect hail. They can see how fast a storm moves. They can track its direction. They can also measure how strong the storm is. Many weather forecasters use radar maps on TV and online.

1964

Year the National Severe Storms Laboratory (NSSL) was officially founded

- The NSSL is a nationwide weather laboratory.
- Experts at NSSL use high-tech radar tools to detect storms.
- Today, weather radar maps are brightly colored. Color was first introduced to the maps in 1975.

What's Going On Up There?

Cumulonimbus clouds.

Hail is produced way up high in the clouds. Hail is usually found in dense, towering clouds. These are called cumulonimbus clouds.

These clouds are famous for making thunderstorms. Some thunderstorms include hail.

All clouds are made up of water vapor. When the air cools,

0.25

Size across in inches (6.4 mm) of a pea-sized piece of hail

- Hail size is usually compared to the size of common objects.
- A few of the sizes are pennies, quarters, golf balls, and tea cups.
- The largest size is grapefruit. It measures 4.5 inches (11.5 cm).

water vapor turns into droplets. Those droplets are rain. When the wind flows up and the air chills, the droplets freeze. They fall through the cloud and are pushed back up again. This happens over and over again. The hailstones grow. They get heavier. These clouds are like factories for hail.

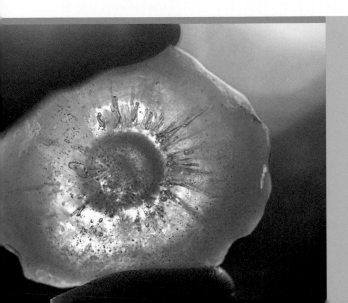

WHAT'S INSIDE HAIL?

When a piece of hail is cut in half, rings are visible. Each ring is a layer of water. A new layer is added each time the hail travels back up through its cloud. The biggest pieces of hail traveled through the cloud many, many times.

What Is Cloud Seeding?

Can people control the weather? The short answer is no, we cannot. But that hasn't stopped people from trying. For thousands of years, humans have tried. The newest idea is called cloud seeding. Cloud seeding is an attempt to change the type or amount of rain, hail, or snow that falls out of clouds. In this process, special substances are added to the air that could help water and ice form more easily. So far, seeding has been used to create more rainfall.

Scientists think cloud seeding could also reduce the amount of

hail that forms in clouds. When clouds are seeded, pieces of ice compete with each other for water. The hailstones don't grow quite as large. As they fall to the ground, they melt. Smaller hail could be good news. However, cloud-seeding programs are still very expensive. We probably won't see a lot of seeding anytime soon.

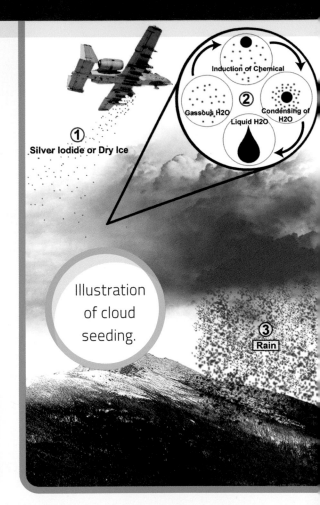

Illustration of cloud seeding.

THINK ABOUT IT

Should humans try to change the weather? What are the pros and cons?

1946
Year of the first cloud-seeding experiments

- The earliest experiments were done in the US.
- Over 50 countries around the world are running cloud-seeding programs.
- Seeding can especially help farmers and residents in dry areas.

Silver iodide flares on the wing of a plane.

21

10

Does Climate Change Affect the Intensity of Hailstorms?

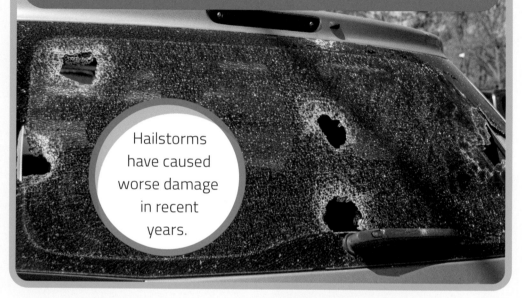

Hailstorms have caused worse damage in recent years.

Some scientists wonder whether climate change is affecting hail. Climate change has been happening on Earth. The planet is warming up. A warmer planet can make it harder for plants and animals to live. Humans are speeding up the change. Many scientists around the world are concerned. They want to slow down or stop the warming. Climate change can affect weather in negative ways. It can produce bad storms.

Experts think that climate change could make hailstorms worse. More updrafts will cause more hail to form. However, warmer weather might help hailstones melt as they fall to Earth. More water in the air could change

Temperature Change in the Last 50 Years

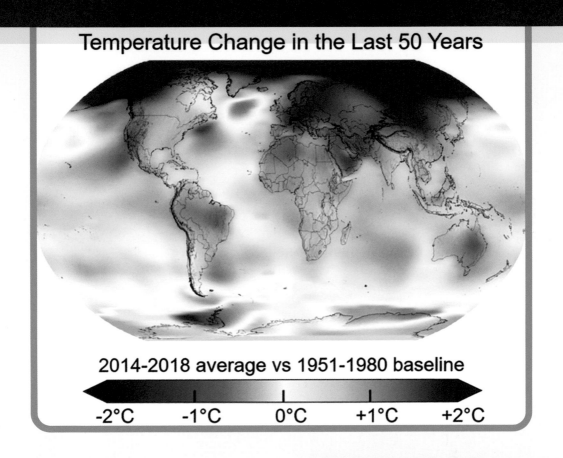

2014-2018 average vs 1951-1980 baseline

| -2°C | -1°C | 0°C | +1°C | +2°C |

hailstones, too. Scientists aren't sure how they will change. Water could produce more hail. It could also make bigger hail. Scientists need more data. Then they will be better able to predict the future of hailstorms.

June 30, 2019

Date of the biggest hailstorm Mexico has ever seen

- In some areas, cars were covered in 6.5 feet (2 m) of hail.
- That June, most days topped 90°F (32°C).
- One of the effects of global warming is extreme weather. Hurricanes and heat waves are just two examples.

11

What Are Some Historic Hailstorms?

Damage after the Sydney, Australia hailstorm, 1999.

Hail isn't new. It has always existed, just like rain and snow. Most storms are mild, but some are extreme. In June 1959, hailstorms in Selden, Kansas, produced 18 inches (45 cm) of hail. The air in Selden became very cold. Temperatures plunged from 80° Fahrenheit (27° C) to 38° Fahrenheit (3° C). This is normal. The hailstones cool off the air as they fall. The storms lasted 85 minutes.

2

Weight in pounds (1 kg) of the heaviest hailstones ever recorded

- These monster hailstones fell on April 14, 1986.
- The storm occurred in Bangladesh.
- The massive hailstones killed 92 people.

In 1999, a huge hailstorm socked Australia. It was the country's costliest storm ever. Baseball-sized hailstones measured 3.5 inches (9 cm) across. More than 35,000 buildings were destroyed. Forty thousand vehicles and 25 airplanes were damaged. The total cost was $1.7 billion.

LEGENDARY HAILSTONES

Many "historic" hailstorms are just stories. One legend tells of an 11-pound hailstone in China in 1986. Another myth features a hailstone the size of an elephant. That one fell on India in the late 18th century. Most likely, some hailstones on the ground stuck together.

Can Hailstorms Kill?

Always take cover during a hailstorm.

Penny-sized hailstones are small. Pea-sized hailstones are even smaller. These don't do much damage. They fall slowly. They melt quickly. Larger hailstones are another matter. Softball-sized and grapefruit-sized hailstones measure several inches across. They can cause injuries. Some people have died during hailstorms.

4

Number of people killed by hail in the US since 2000

- It is very rare for a hailstorm to cause death.
- About 24 people are injured by hail in the US each year.
- Usually, those who get hurt are out in the open. Golfers and farmers are at risk of being struck.

One of the worst-ever hailstorms hit India on April 30, 1888. A total of 246 people lost their lives. Some were hit by hail, while others were buried under it. Hundreds of cattle and sheep also died in the storm. People reported hail the size of goose eggs and oranges.

BLACK MONDAY

The deadliest hailstorm occurred on April 13, 1360. A sudden hailstorm killed an estimated 1,000 English soldiers. They were fighting in Chartres, France, during the Hundred Years' War. They took it as a sign of God's displeasure with the war. The day has long been called "Black Monday" because it was so terrible.

Staying Safe in a Hailstorm

While most hailstorms are mild, some can be dangerous. Here are a few key ways to keep yourself, your friends, and your family safe during a hailstorm:

- Stay indoors and away from glass.

- Close drapes and blinds to reduce risk of injury from broken glass.

- Have flashlights and extra batteries close by in case of power outages.

- When driving, pull into a covered area, such as a gas station.

- Angle your car so the hailstones hit the thick front windshield instead of other windows.

- If you are outside with no available shelter close by, crouch down, turn away from the wind, cover your head and neck with your hands. This will better protect you from hailstones and other debris.

- Avoid trees, towers, metal fences and poles in order to reduce your risk of being struck by lightning.

- Avoid flooded areas.

Glossary

atmosphere
The layer or layers of gases surrounding a planet.

climate change
Major changes in the normal temperature and weather conditions over a long period of time.

cumulonimbus
The towering clouds with flat tops that often bring heavy rain or thunderstorms.

debris
The broken pieces of structures, vehicles, and plants left after a destructive hailstorm.

erosion
The process of being broken down by wind, water, or other forms of nature.

hazardous
The dangerous conditions after a destructive hailstorm has wreaked havoc.

meteorologists
People trained in the science of the atmosphere and weather forecasting.

precipitation
The weather condition in which something such as rain, snow, sleet, or hail falls from the sky.

radar
A system for detecting weather by sending out waves that reflect off precipitation.

weather balloon
A balloon equipped with tools that is sent into the atmosphere to gather information about the weather.

Read More

Drimmer, Stephanie Warren. *National Geographic Kids Ultimate Weatherpedia*. Washington, DC: National Geographic Kids, 2019.

Ganeri, Anita. *Earth in 30 Seconds*. New York, NY: Quarter Publishing Group USA, 2016.

Marsico, Katie. *Weather Math*. Minneapolis, MN: Lerner Publishing Group, 2016.

Ransom, Candice. *Investigating the Water Cycle*. Minneapolis, MN: Lerner Publishing Group, 2016.

Visit 12StoryLibrary.com

Scan the code or use your school's login at **12StoryLibrary.com** for recent updates about this topic and a full digital version of this book. Enjoy free access to:

- Digital ebook
- Breaking news updates
- Live content feeds
- Videos, interactive maps, and graphics
- Additional web resources

Note to educators: Visit 12StoryLibrary.com/register to sign up for free premium website access. Enjoy live content plus a full digital version of every 12-Story Library book you own for every student at your school.

Index

About the Author

Kaitlyn Duling was born in Illinois but now resides in Washington, DC. Kaitlyn has written over 80 books for children and teens. You can learn more about her at www.kaitlynduling.com.

READ MORE FROM 12-STORY LIBRARY

Every 12-Story Library Book is available in many formats. For more information, visit **12StoryLibrary.com**